JAZZ PIANO
SCALES AND EXERCISES

By Lee Evans

ISBN: 978-1-5400-3257-7

Visit Hal Leonard Online at
www.halleonard.com

Contact Us:
Hal Leonard
7777 West Bluemound Road
Milwaukee, WI 53213
Email: info@halleonard.com

In Europe contact:
Hal Leonard Europe Limited
42 Wigmore Street
Marylebone, London, W1U 2RN
Email: info@halleonardeurope.com

In Australia contact:
Hal Leonard Australia Pty. Ltd.
4 Lentara Court
Cheltenham, Victoria, 3192 Australia
Email: info@halleonard.com.au

ABOUT THE AUTHOR

Lee Evans, professor of music and former chairperson of the Theater and Fine Arts Department at New York City's Pace University, graduated from NYC's High School of Music & Art and completed degrees at New York University and Columbia University, receiving his Master of Arts and Doctor of Education from the latter. In addition to college-level teaching, he also taught briefly at both the junior high and high school levels. Professionally, he concertized for ten consecutive seasons under the auspices of Columbia Arts Management, and has performed on some the world's most prestigious stages, including the White House. He has also served as music coordinator/director for Tom Jones; Engelbert Humperdinck; Carol Channing; Cat Stevens; and Emerson, Lake & Palmer.

Dr. Evans is an acclaimed educator, lecturer, performer, composer, and arranger, and is the author of innumerable articles in educational journals and music magazines, as well as over 100 books in the United States, 38 in Japan, and two in Russia. He has demonstrated that it is possible for classical teachers with no prior jazz experience to teach and include jazz concepts in the classical lesson. He has succeeded in bringing an understanding of – and feeling for – jazz to keyboard students and teachers worldwide.

CONTENTS

INTRODUCTION

Diatonic scales have been the tonal foundation of Western music from the 17th through the 19th centuries and much of the music of the 20th and 21st centuries. These scales are used in harmonic analysis – the study of functions and relationships of chords – and are the basis for structuring chords. Scale passages appear in almost all types of music with such regular frequency that it is imperative for pianists to master their performance. Furthermore, the practice of scales is important for the development of finger independence and control.

A **diatonic scale** is a series of five whole-steps and two half-steps that proceeds up or down the staff, alternating line-space-line-space. A diatonic scale has no chromatic tones, neither repeating nor omitting a letter of the musical alphabet (A-B-C-D-E-F-G) in sequence. Major and minor scales are diatonic scales.

A **key** is major or minor depending upon whether it is based on a major or minor scale.

The jazz-oriented exercises in this book are based on major scales, melodic minor scales, and harmonic minor scales. (Natural minor scales, which are modal in quality, are not ordinarily practiced by pianists during the course of their training; hence, they are not included among the exercises in this book. They are mentioned, however, because of their importance in understanding theory.) In each jazz exercise, the scales appear in somewhat disguised fashion.

A **major scale** always has the following sequence of whole-steps and half-steps:

C Major Scale

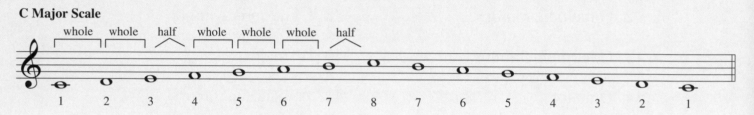

To form a natural minor scale from a major scale:

- Ascending: lower the 3rd, 6th, and 7th degrees of the major scale by one half-step.

- Descending: same notes as ascending.

C Natural Minor Scale

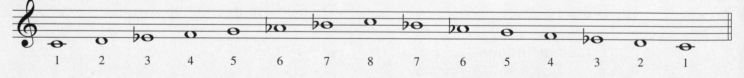

C minor scales have a key signature of three flats, the same key signature as E♭ major. These scales are therefore said to be related. C minor is the relative minor of E♭ major. To ascertain which minor key is related to a given major key, locate the 6th degree of the major scale. (For example: In the key of C major, A is the 6th degree. The scale of A minor has the same key signature – no sharps or flats – as C major. Therefore, A minor is the relative minor of C major.)

As stated earlier, **minor scales** – like major scales – are **diatonic scales** in that they have five whole-steps and two half-steps; they use the next alphabet letter, without omitting or repeating an alphabet letter. The notes are written in succession on the next available staff line or space, without omitting or repeating a staff line or space.

A **minor scale** always has the sequence of whole-steps and half-steps shown below. Notice that the half-steps occur only between scale steps 2-3 and 5-6. Here is the A natural minor scale; it uses the same pitches descending as ascending.

A Natural Minor Scale

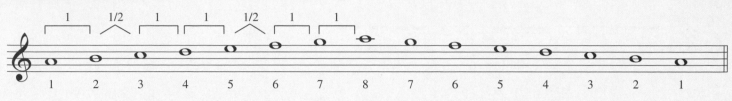

In a **major scale**, the interval of a half-step occurs between scale degrees 7 and 8. When the 7th scale degree is only a half-step away from the tonic tone, the 7th degree is then called a **leading tone** because there is a strong sense of urgency for it to lead to, or move to, the tonic note.

In a **minor scale**, however, the interval of a whole-step, rather than one half-step, occurs between scale degrees 7 and 8. Thus, there is a much less compelling sense of movement from the 7th scale degree to the tonic tone. Composers liked the minor scale a lot, but were dismayed by that one aspect of it: the whole-step distance between scale steps 7 and 8. As a result, composers created two altered minor scales that would correct that perceived "flaw." The unaltered version of the minor scale thus came to be known as the **natural minor scale**, the term "natural" in this context meaning "pure," or unaltered. The two altered minor scales came to be known, respectively, as **harmonic minor** and **melodic minor**.

The **harmonic minor scale** raises the 7th note of the natural minor scale one half-step and uses the same pitches descending as ascending.

Note: The key signature employed for the harmonic minor scale is that of the natural minor scale. The raised 7th pitch in this altered scale uses an accidental within the body of any music based on this scale.

A Harmonic Minor Scale

The **melodic minor scale** is unusual in that it uses different pitches descending than it does ascending. Ascending, the 6th and 7th notes of the natural minor scale are each raised one half-step. Descending, however, those raised pitches are lowered one half-step each, thus restoring them back to the pitches of the original natural minor scale.

Note: The key signature employed for the melodic minor scale is that of the natural minor scale. The raised pitches in this altered scale use an accidental within the body of any music based on this scale.

A Melodic Minor Scale

PRACTICE INSTRUCTIONS

To better understand syncopated rhythms, it is helpful to count aloud while practicing.

For best results, the counting of a composition using predominantly eighth notes should be:

For a work containing mostly 16th notes, the counting should be:

The exercises in this book should be practiced at gradually faster tempos, using a metronome, placing special emphasis on slow practice for greater control. Tempo indications above each jazz exercise represent tempos at which these pieces were conceived by the composer.

All the notes in each exercise should be played at an equal dynamic level, except where accents or other variations in dynamics are indicated.

The sustain (damper) pedal should be used only where indicated.

Thumbs should never hang off the keyboard.

C Major Scale

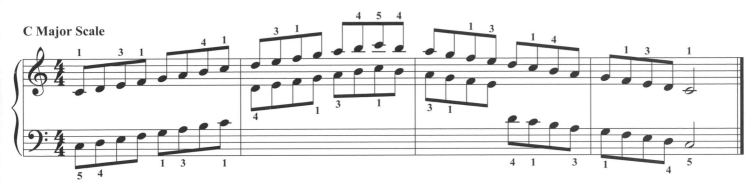

C Major Jazz Exercises

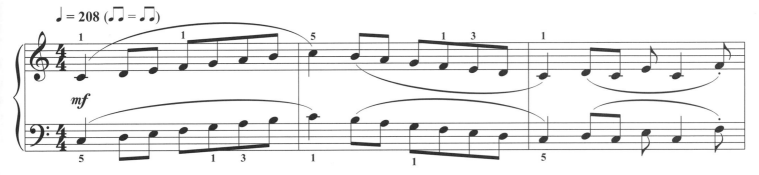

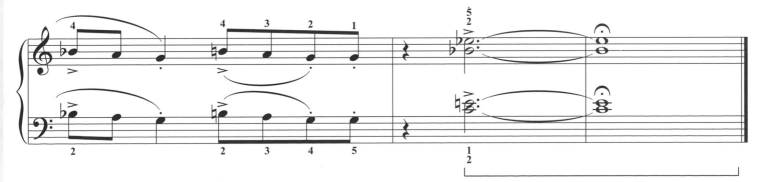

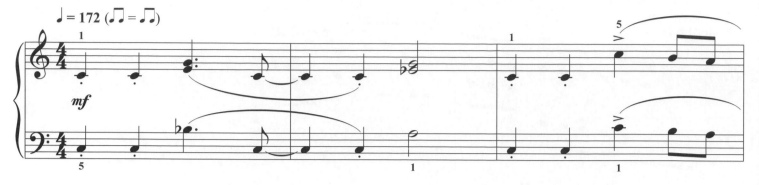

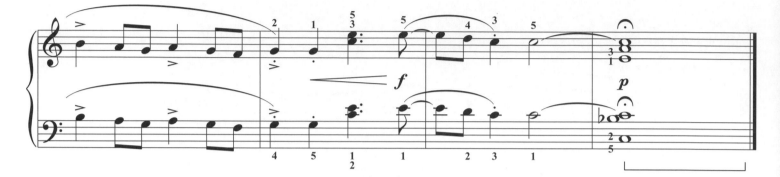

C Melodic Minor Scale

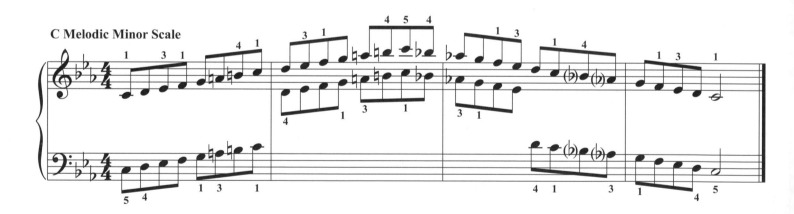

C Melodic Minor Jazz Exercises

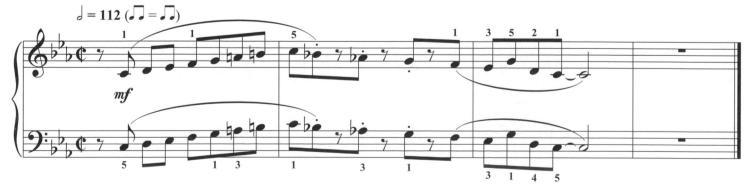

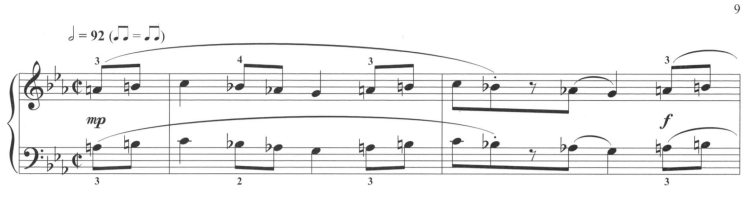

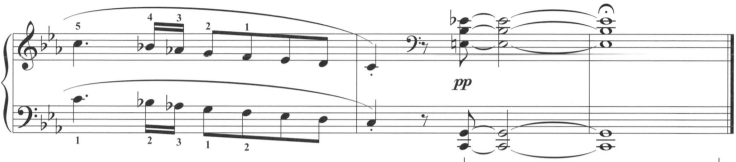

C Harmonic Minor Scale

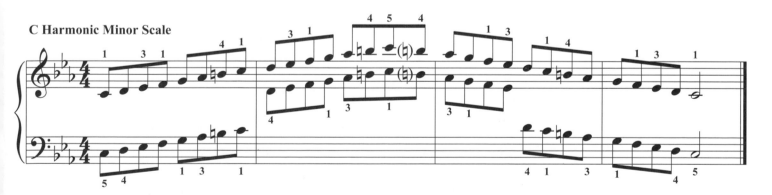

C Harmonic Minor Jazz Exercises

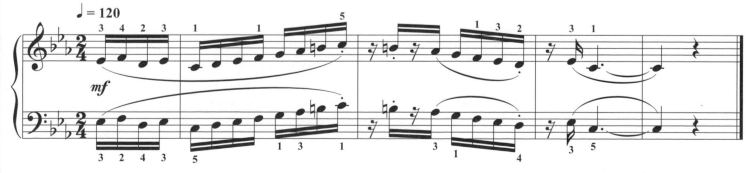

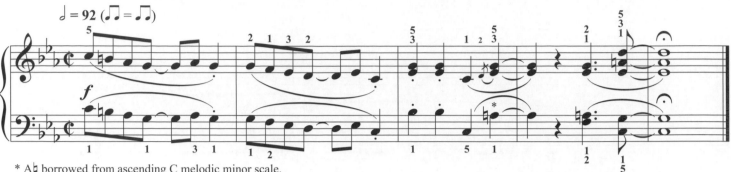

* A♮ borrowed from ascending C melodic minor scale.

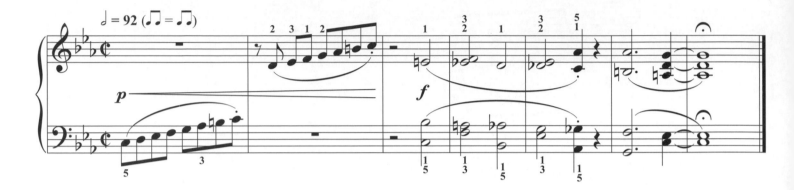

G Major Scale

G Major Jazz Exercises

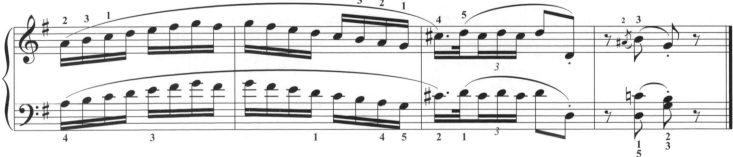

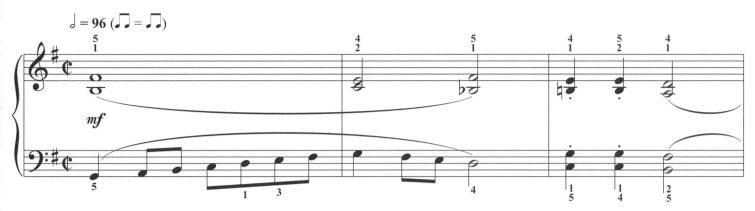

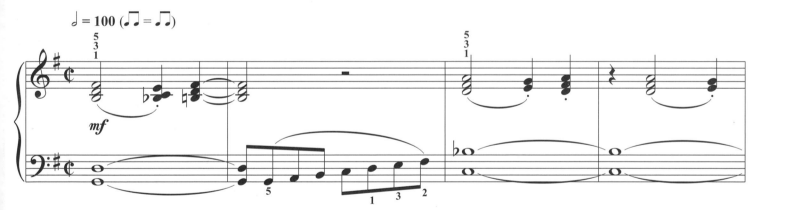

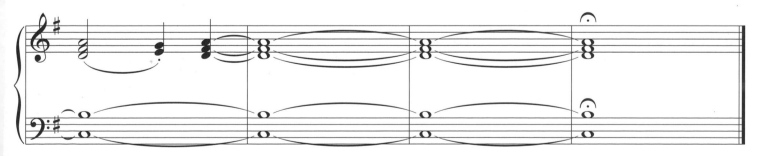

G Melodic Minor Scale

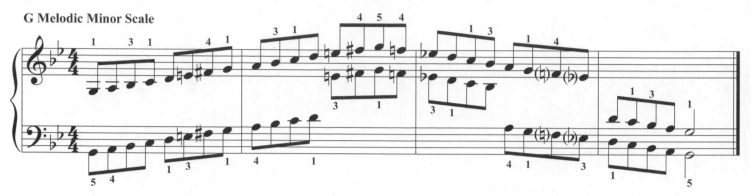

G Melodic Minor Jazz Exercises

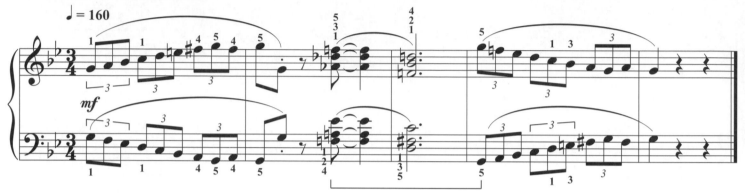

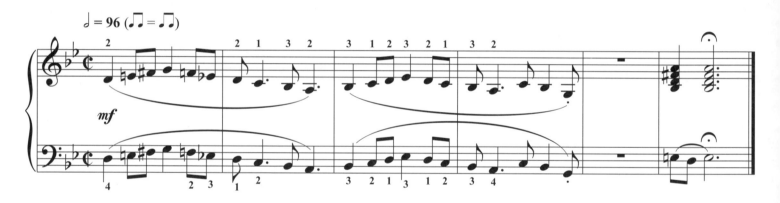

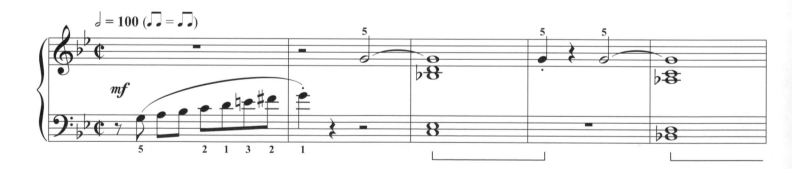

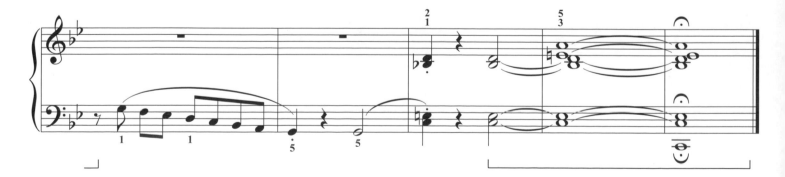

G Harmonic Minor Scale

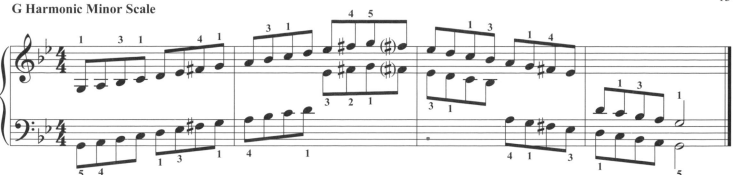

G Harmonic Minor Jazz Exercises

Augmentation (enlarging of time values)

* Right thumb in front of left thumb.

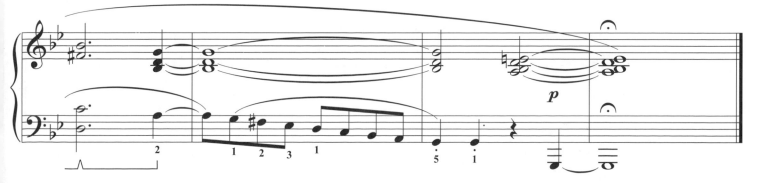

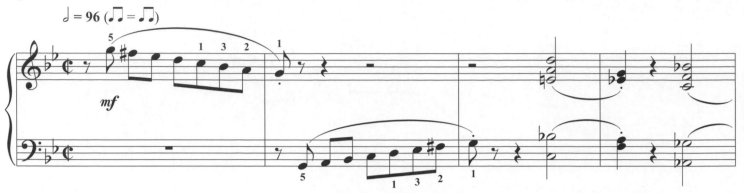

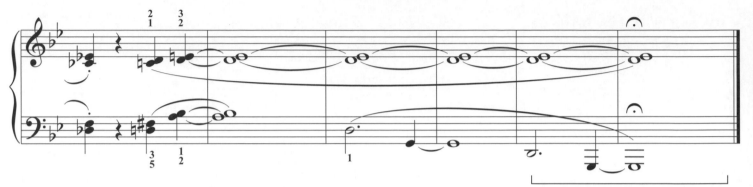

D Major Scale

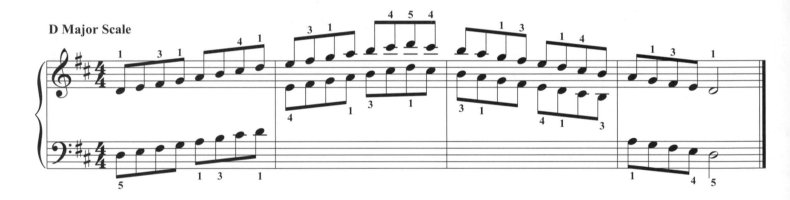

D Major Jazz Exercises

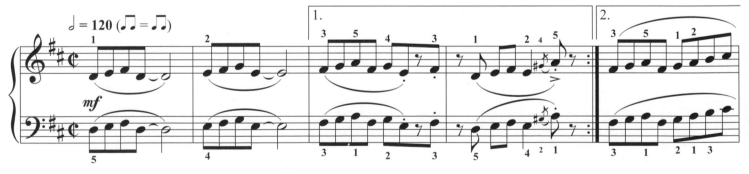

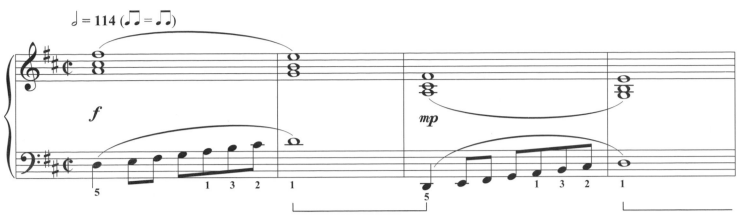

D Melodic Minor Scale

D Melodic Minor Jazz Exercises

♩ = 116 (♫ = ♫)

♩ = 100 (♫ = ♫)

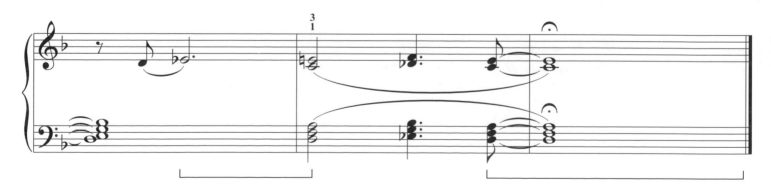

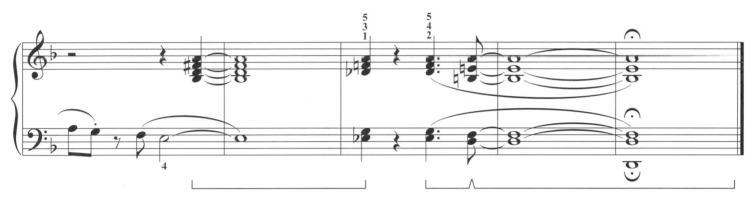

D Harmonic Minor Scale

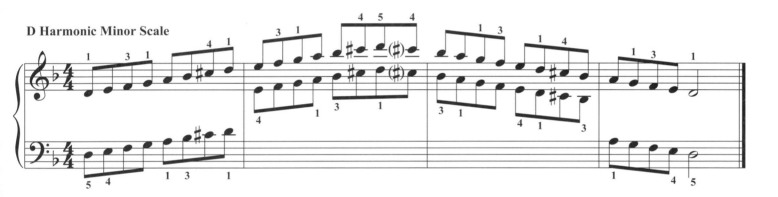

D Harmonic Minor Jazz Exercises

* B♮ borrowed from ascending D melodic minor scale.

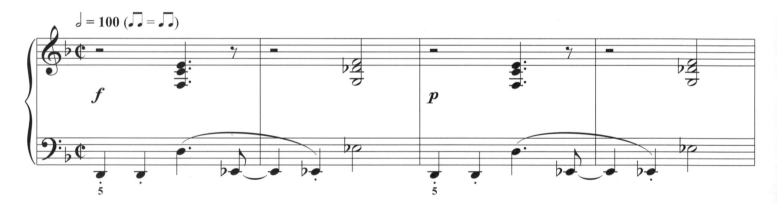

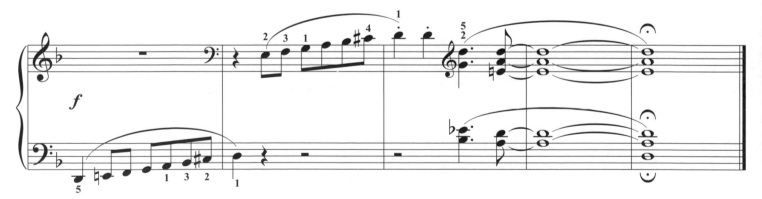

A Major Scale

A Major Jazz Exercises

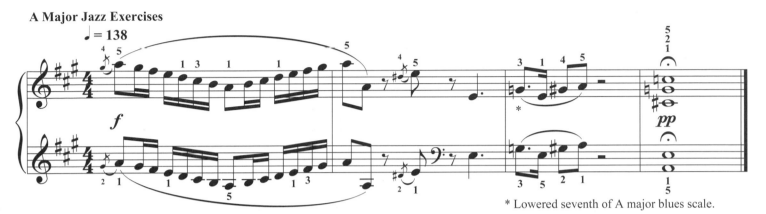

* Lowered seventh of A major blues scale.

* A blues scale is derived from a major scale, using altered scale tones called blue notes, created by lowering the 3rd, 5th, and 7th degrees of the major scale by one half-step.

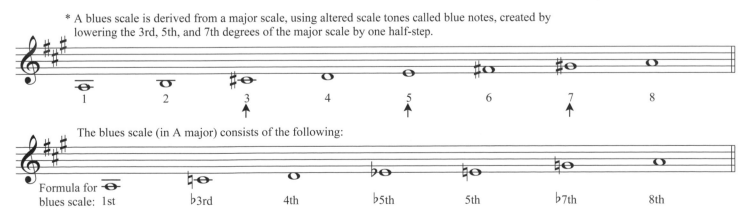

The blues scale (in A major) consists of the following:

Formula for blues scale: 1st   b3rd   4th   b5th   5th   b7th   8th

(Students should practice transposing the blues scale into different keys.)

A Melodic Minor Scale

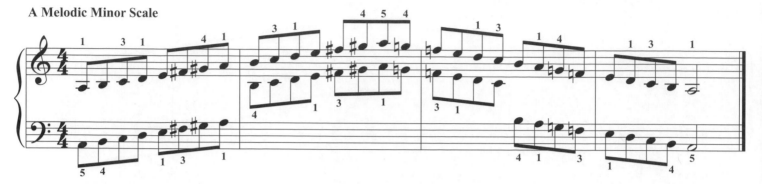

A Melodic Minor Jazz Exercises

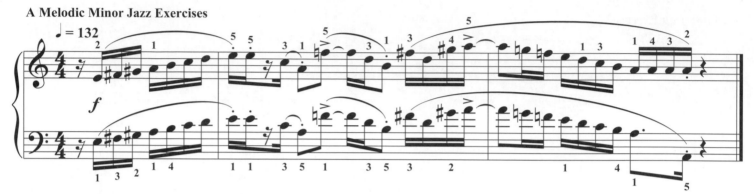

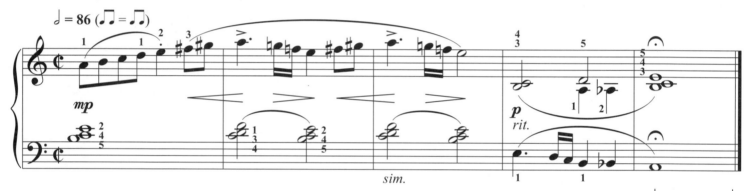

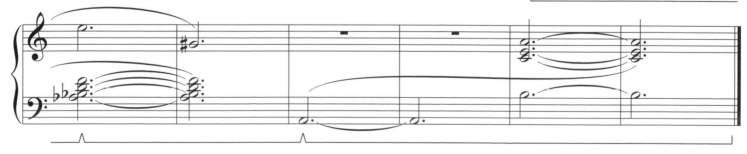

A Harmonic Minor Scale

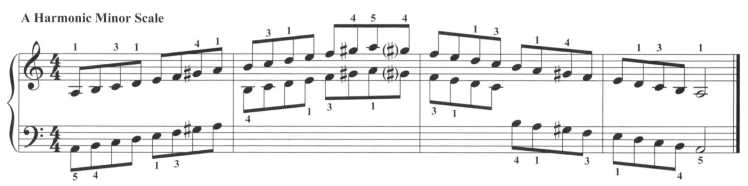

A Harmonic Minor Jazz Exercises

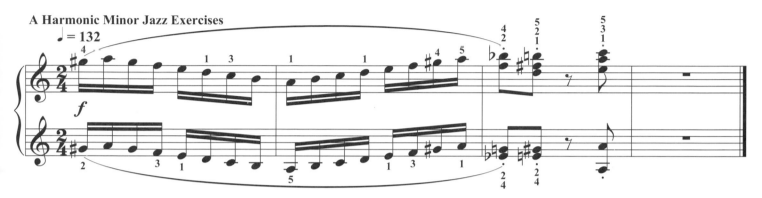

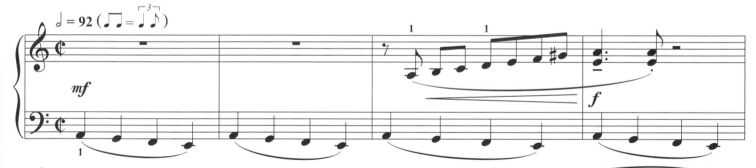

E Major Scale

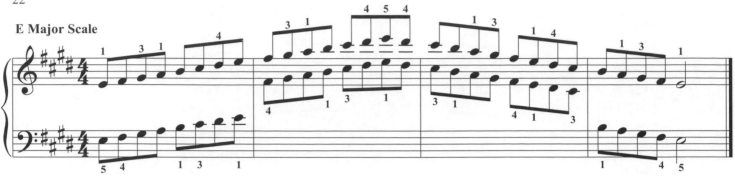

E Major Jazz Exercises

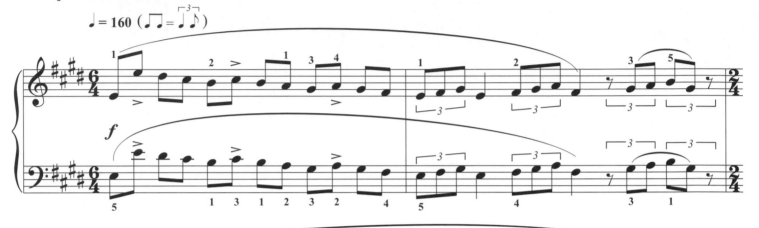

E Melodic Minor Scale

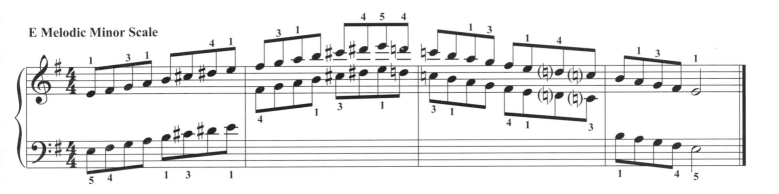

E Melodic Minor Jazz Exercises

* Flatted 5th of the E minor scale.

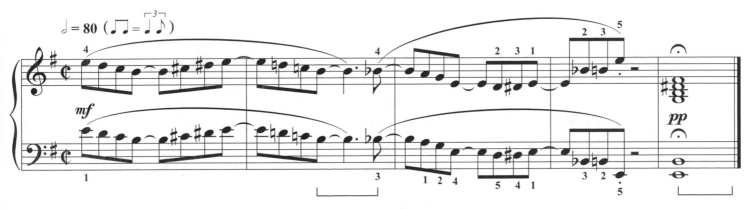

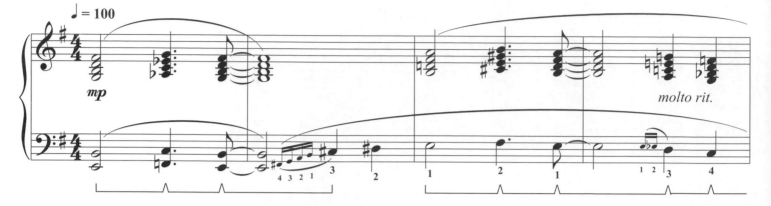

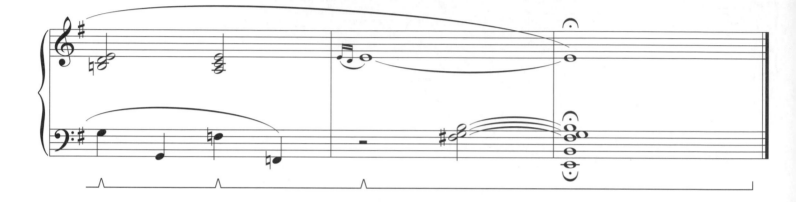

E Harmonic Minor Scale

E Harmonic Minor Jazz Exercises

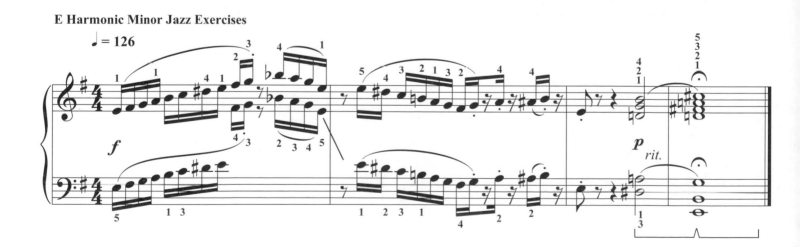

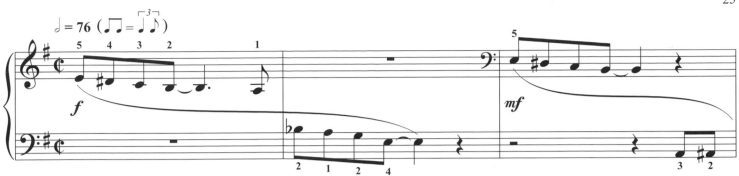

B Major Scale

B Major Jazz Exercises

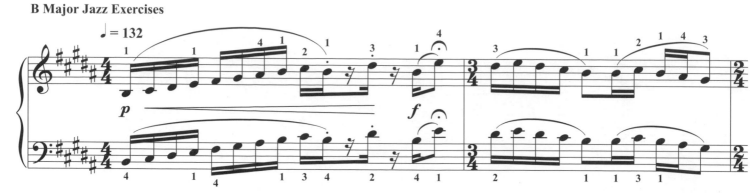

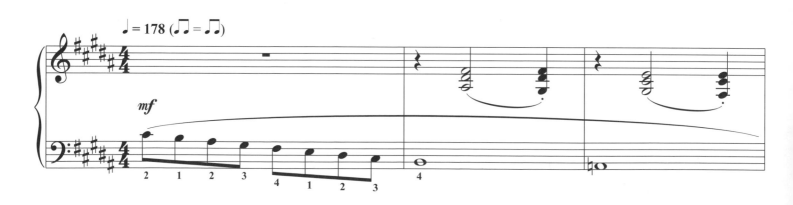

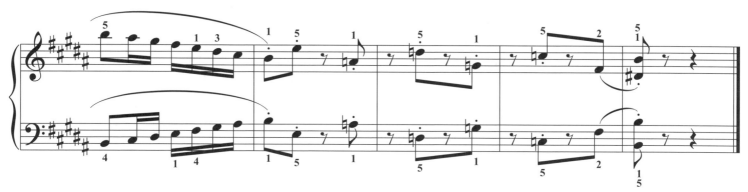

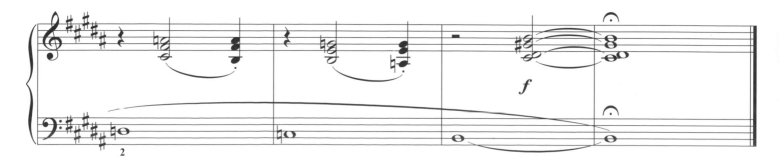

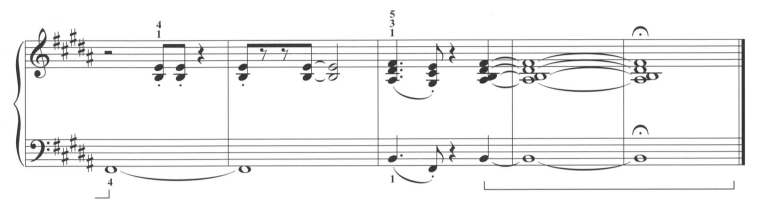

B Melodic Minor Scale

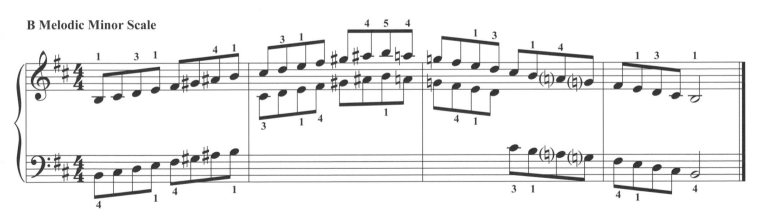

B Melodic Minor Jazz Exercises

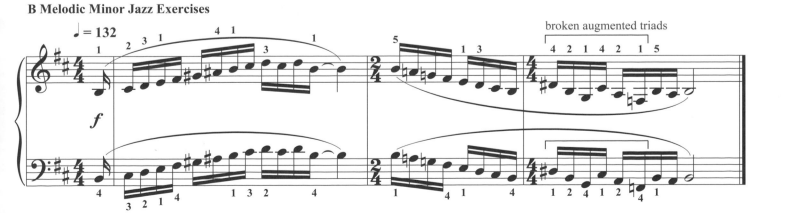

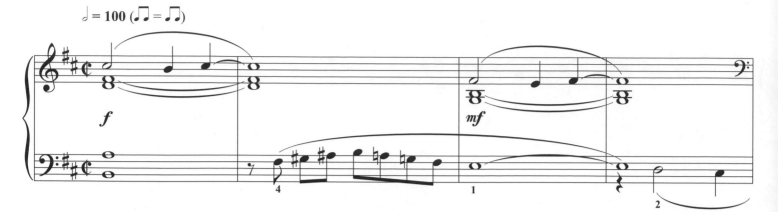

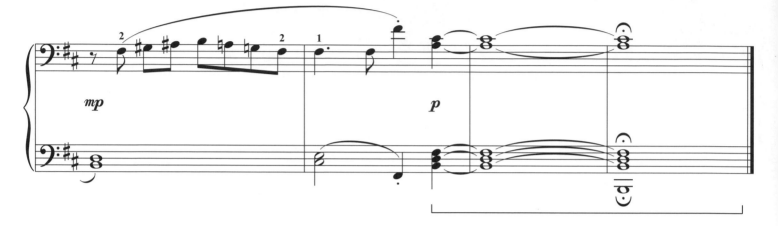

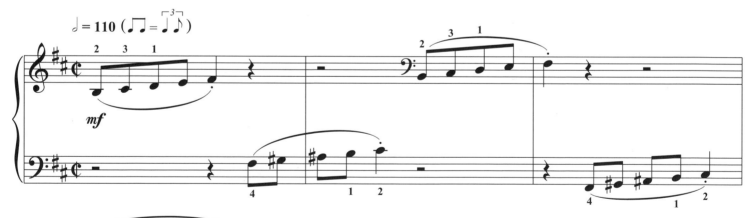

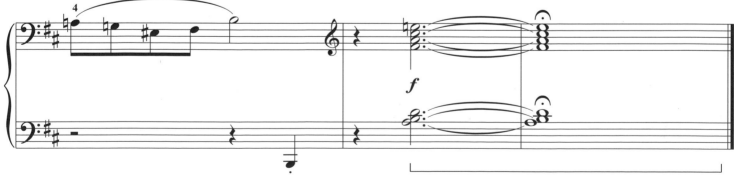

B Harmonic Minor Scale

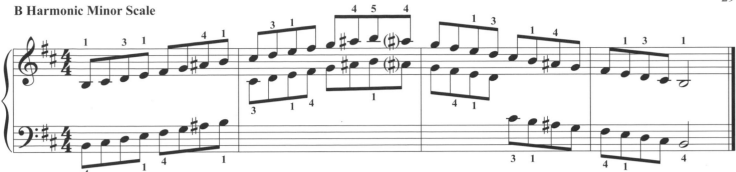

B Harmonic Minor Jazz Exercises

* Lowered fifth degree of B minor scale.

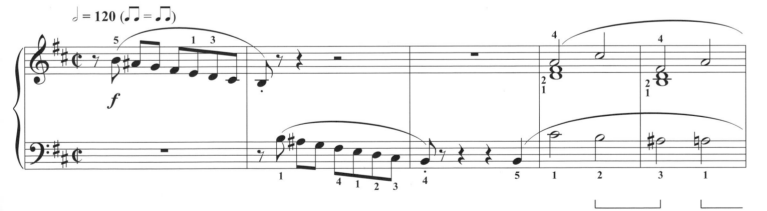

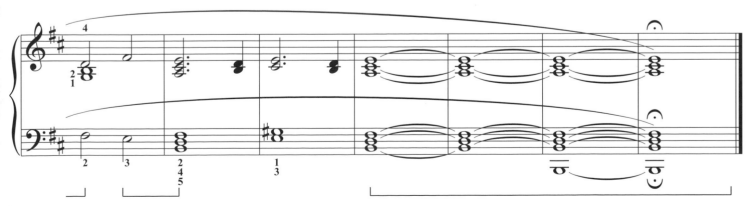

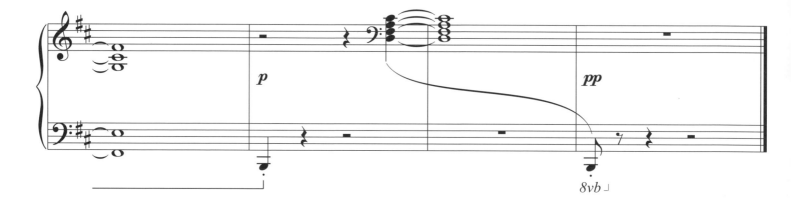

F# Major Scale

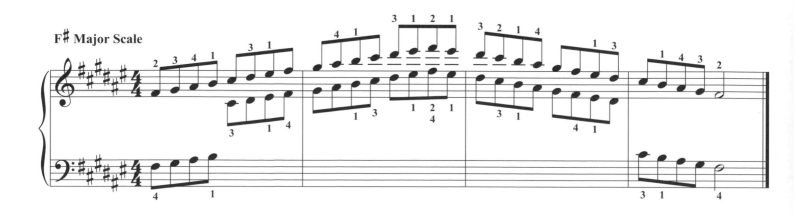

F♯ Major Jazz Exercises (same enharmonically as G♭ Major)

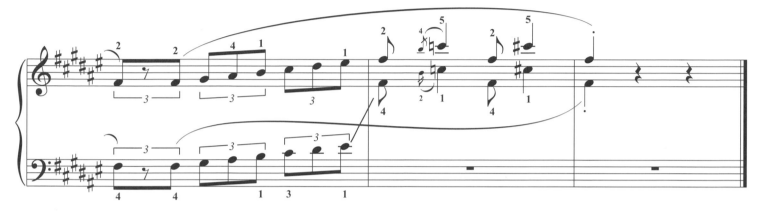

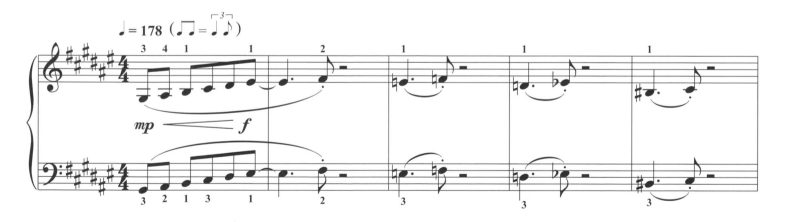

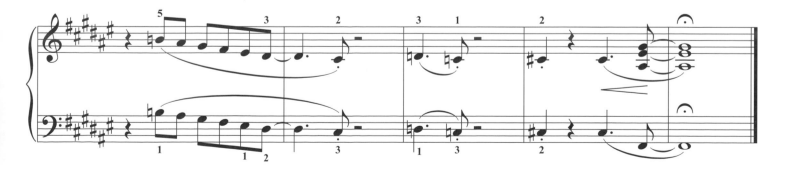

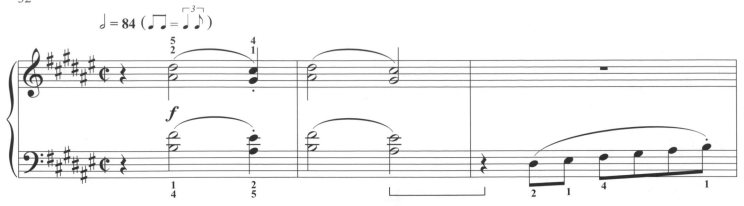

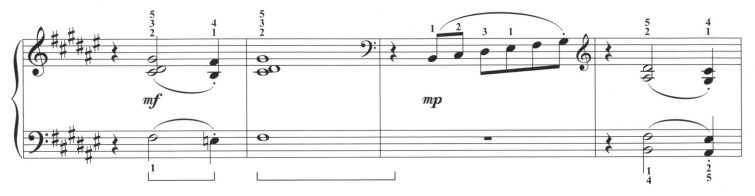

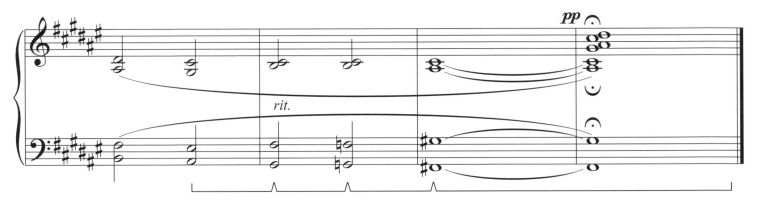

F♯ Melodic Minor Scale

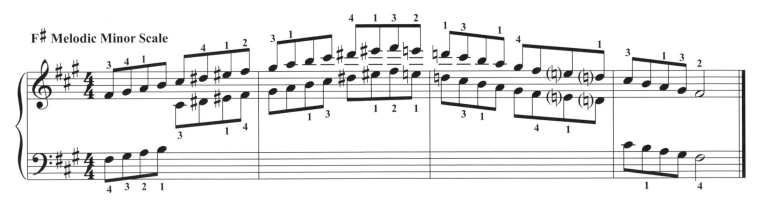

F♯ Melodic Minor Jazz Exercises

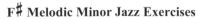

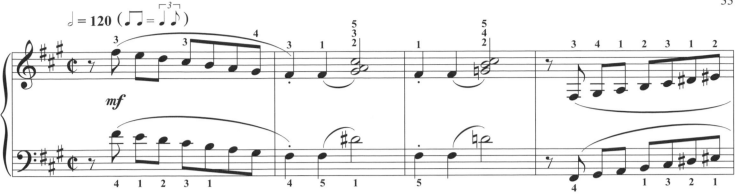

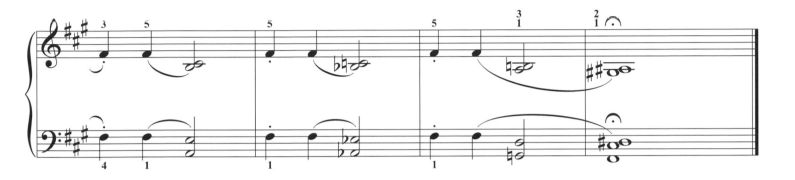

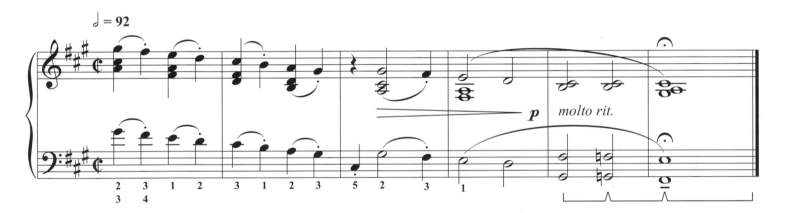

F♯ Harmonic Minor Scale

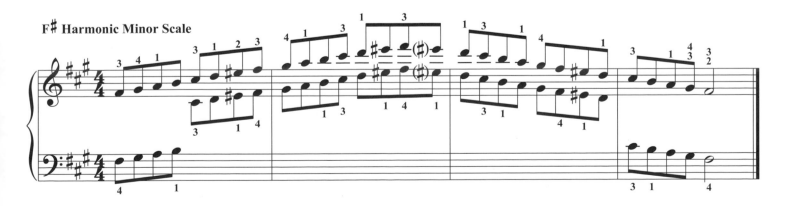

F♯ Harmonic Minor Jazz Exercises

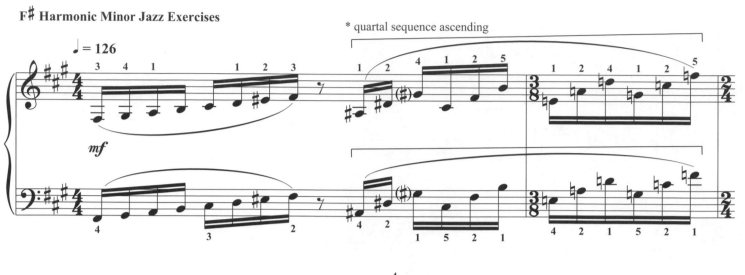

* quartal sequence ascending

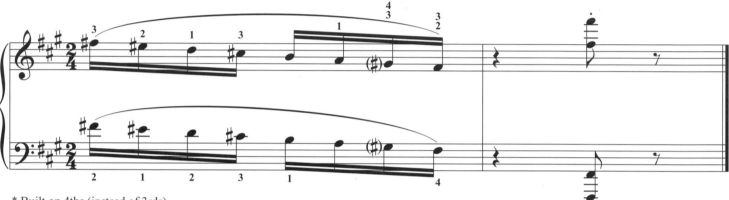

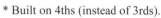

* Built on 4ths (instead of 3rds).

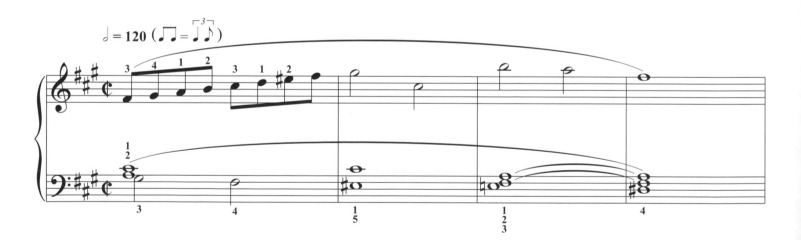

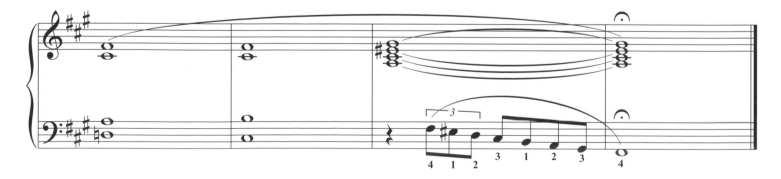

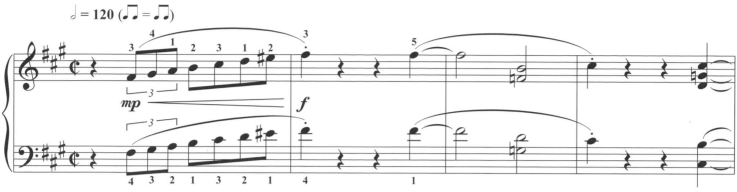

C♯ Major Scale (same enharmonically as D♭ Major)

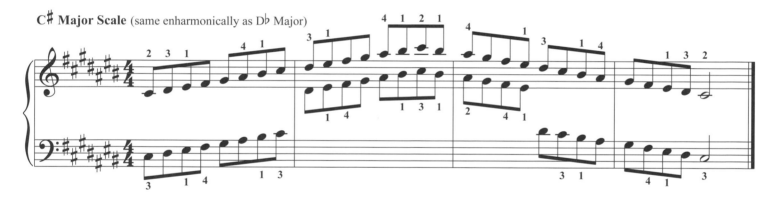

C♯ Major Jazz Exercises (same enharmonically as D♭ Major)

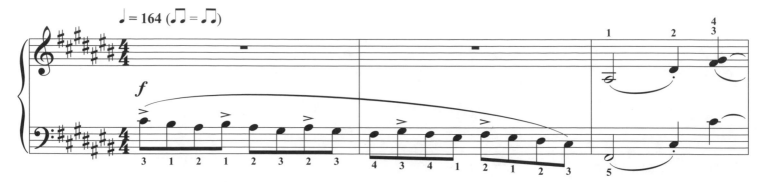

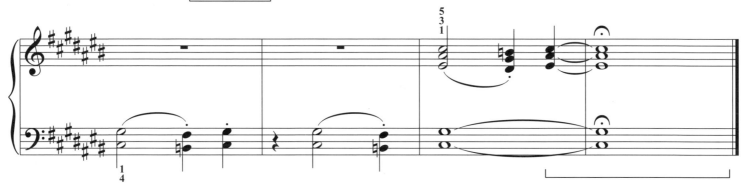

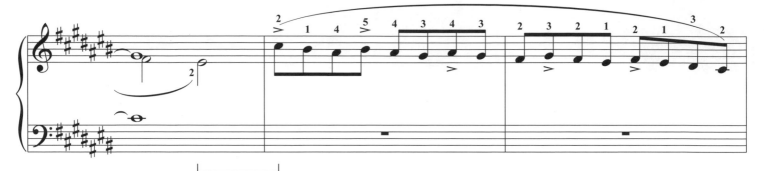

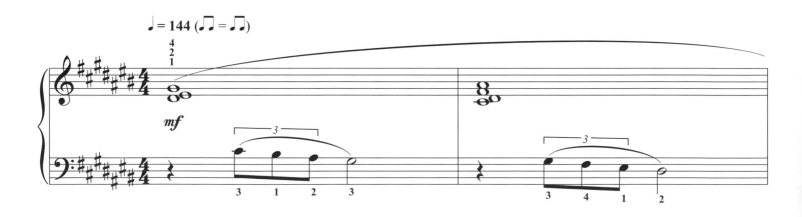

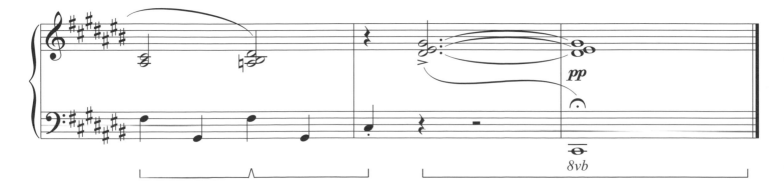

C♯ Melodic Minor Scale

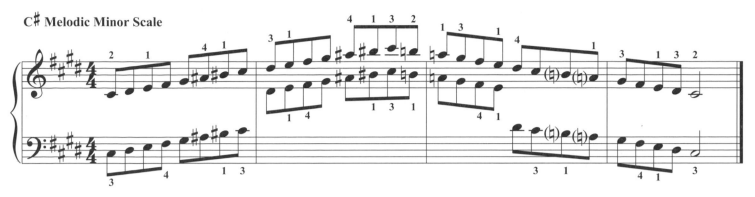

C♯ Melodic Minor Jazz Exercises

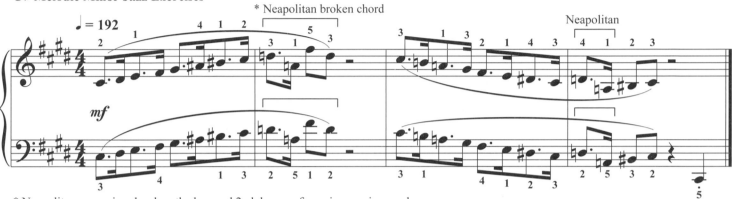

* Neapolitan = a major chord on the lowered 2nd degree of a major or minor scale.

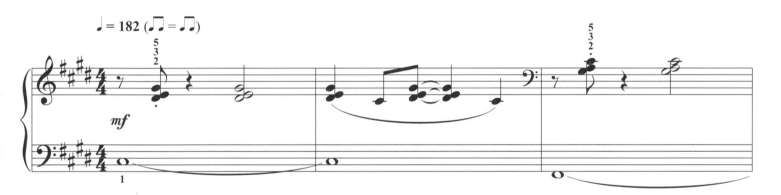

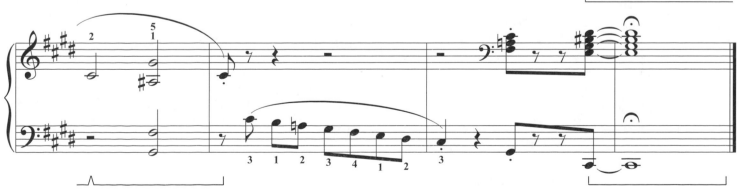

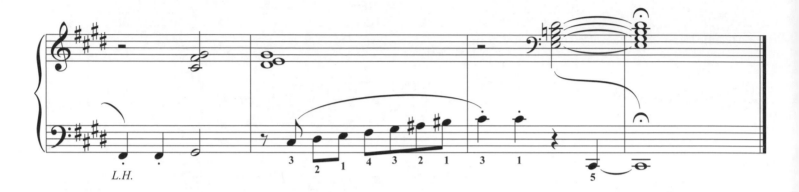

C♯ Harmonic Minor Scale

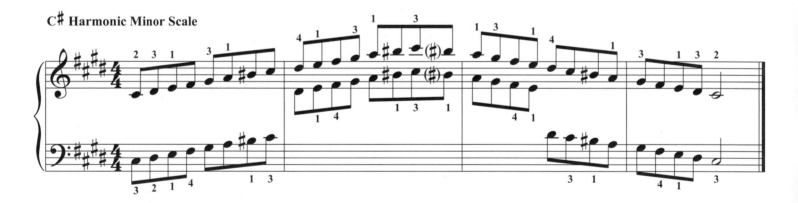

C♯ Harmonic Minor Jazz Exercises

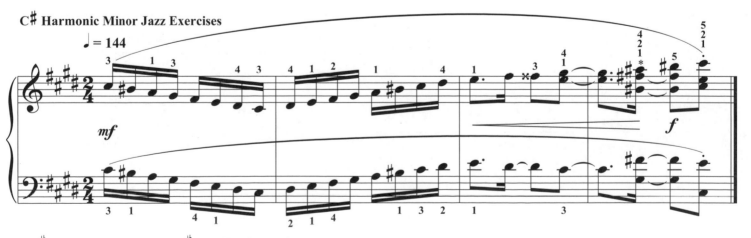

* A♯ borrowed from ascending C♯ melodic minor scale.

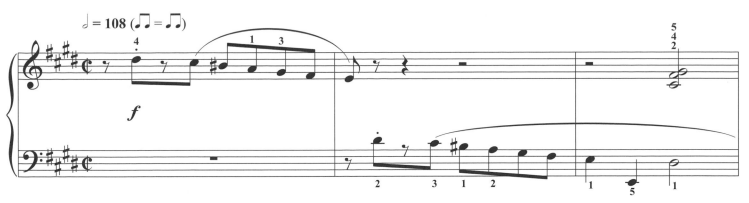

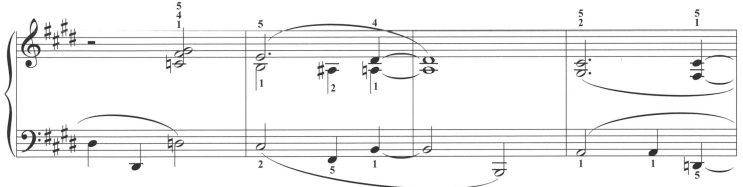

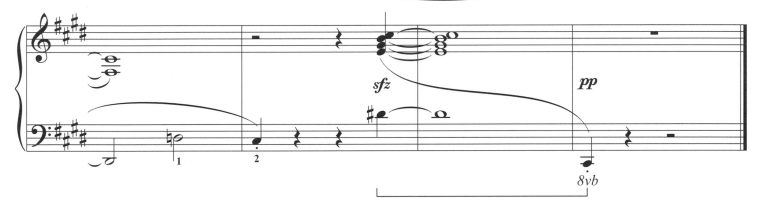

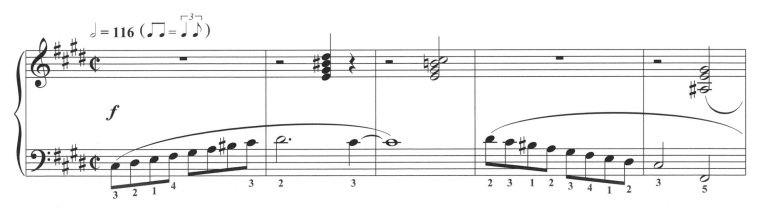

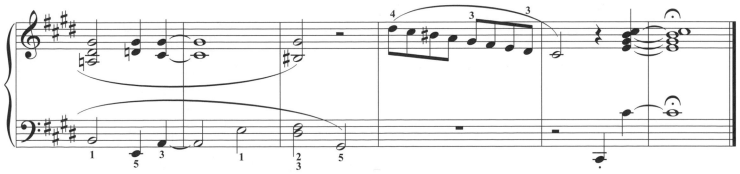

A♭ Major Scale

A♭ Major Jazz Exercises

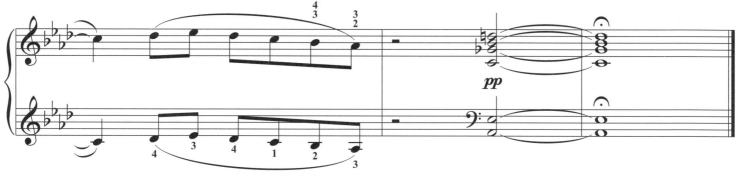

Ab Melodic Minor Scale (same enharmonically as G♯ Melodic Minor)

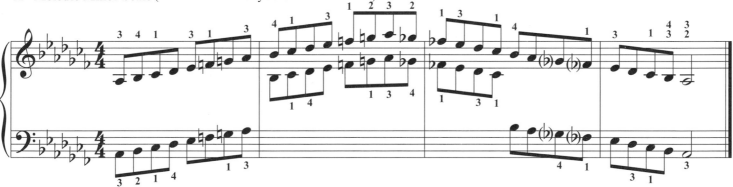

Ab Melodic Minor Jazz Exercises (same enharmonically as G♯ Melodic Minor)

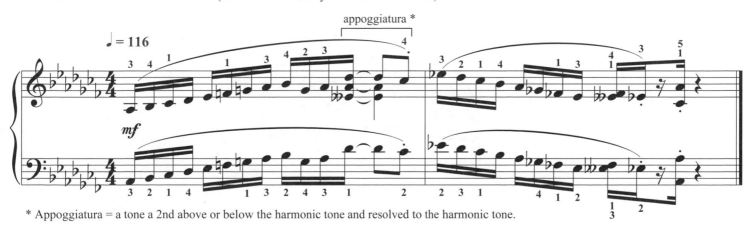

* Appoggiatura = a tone a 2nd above or below the harmonic tone and resolved to the harmonic tone.

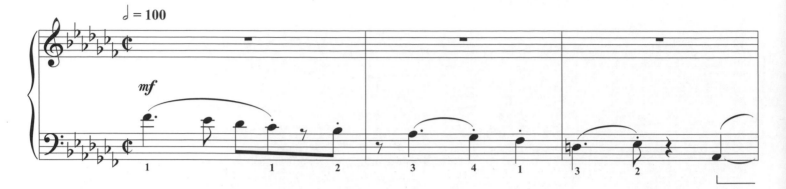

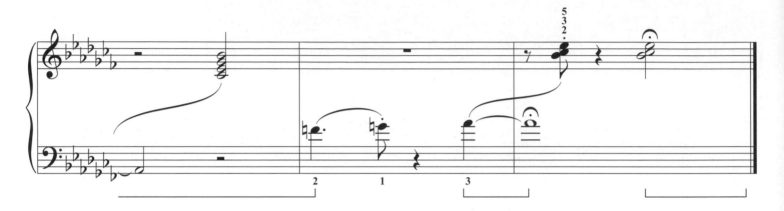

A♭ Harmonic Minor Scale (same enharmonically as G♯ Harmonic Minor)

A♭ Harmonic Minor Jazz Exercises (same enharmonically as G♯ Harmonic Minor)

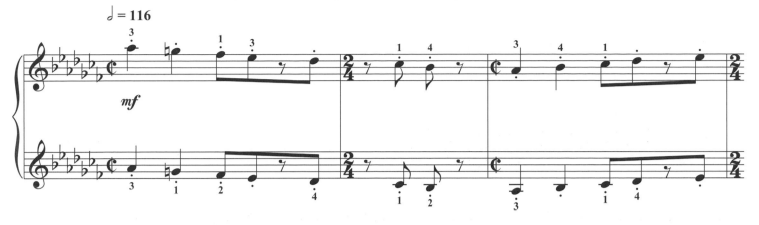

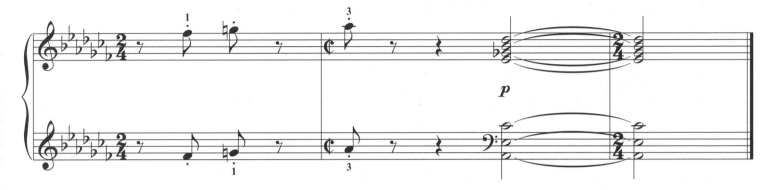

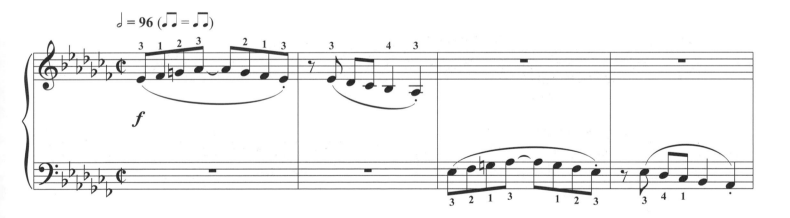

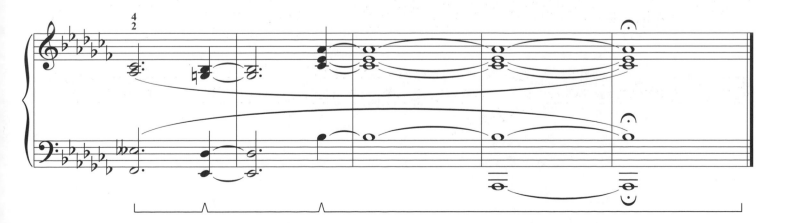

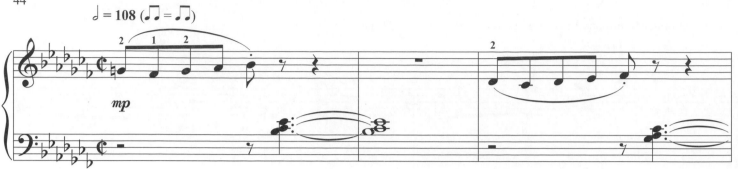

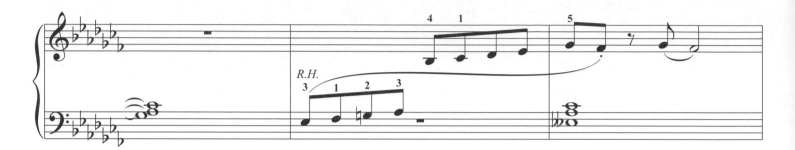

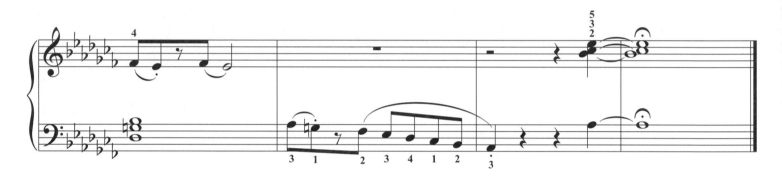

E♭ Major Scale

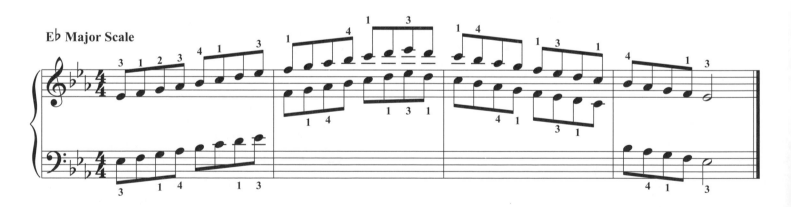

E♭ Major Jazz Exercises

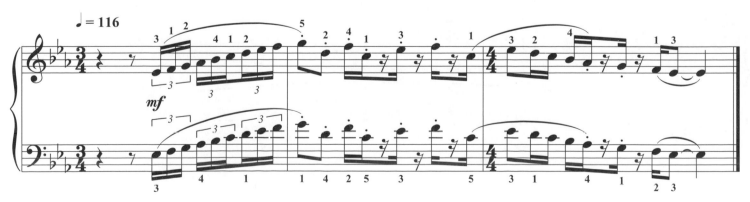

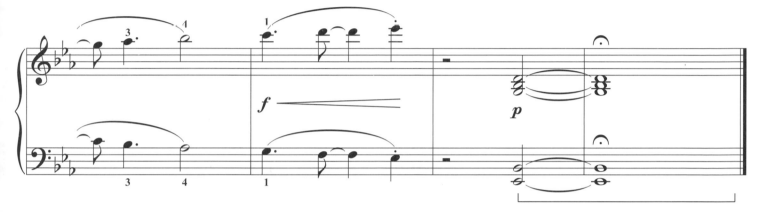
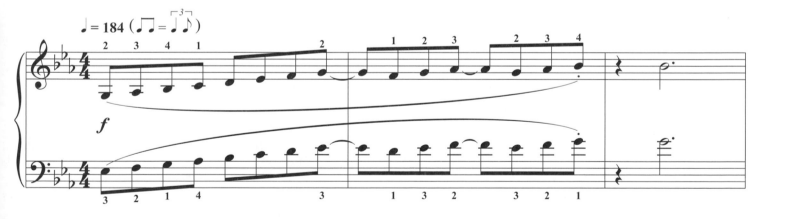
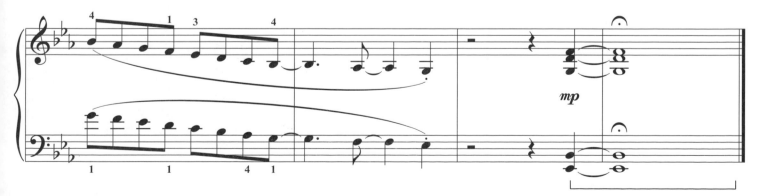

46

E♭ Melodic Minor Scale (same enharmonically as D♯ Melodic Minor)

E♭ Melodic Minor Jazz Exercises (same enharmonically as D♯ Melodic Minor)

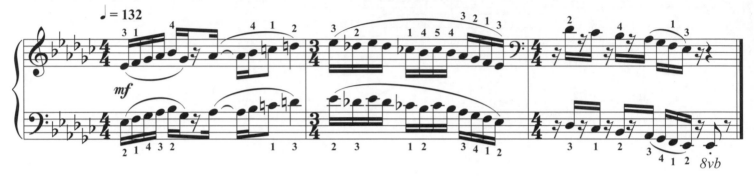

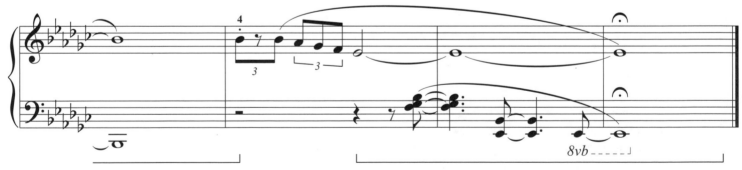

E♭ Harmonic Minor Scale (same enharmonically as D♯ Harmonic Minor)

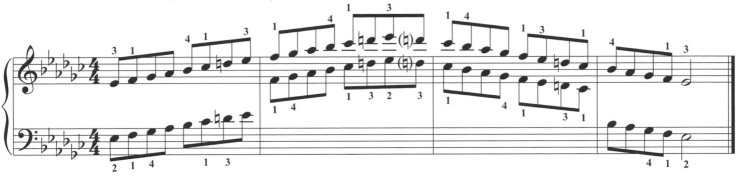

E♭ Harmonic Minor Jazz Exercises (same enharmonically as D♯ Harmonic Minor)

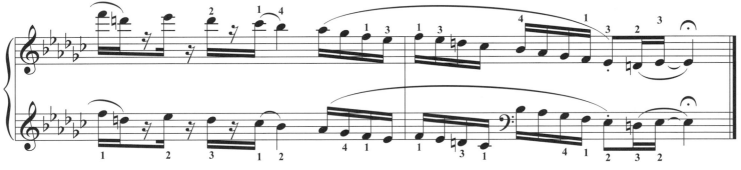

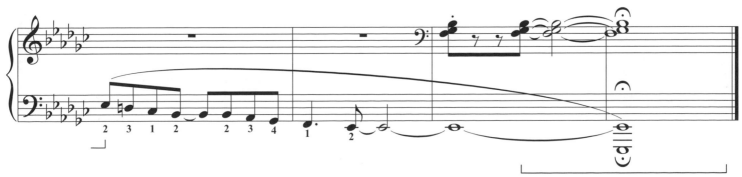

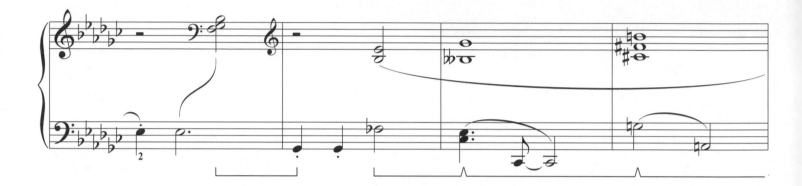

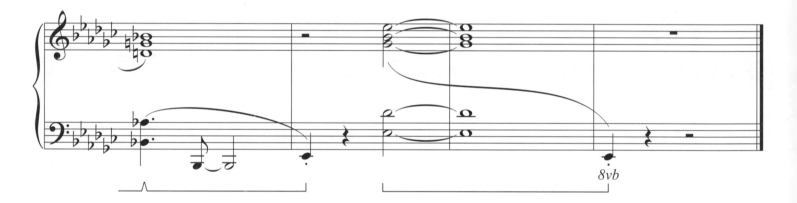

B♭ Major Scale

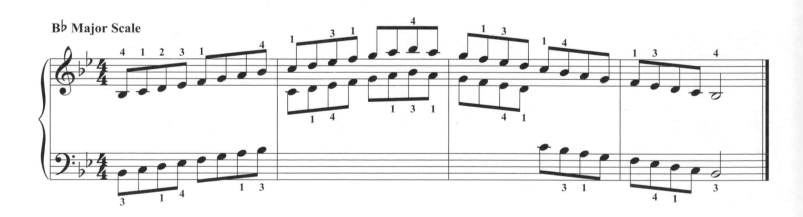

B♭ Major Jazz Exercises

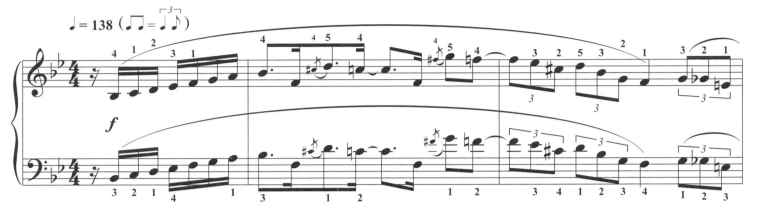

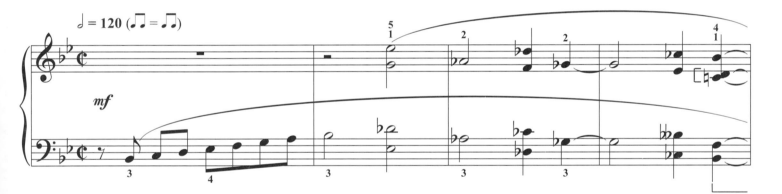

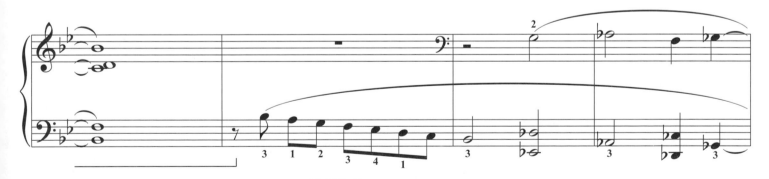

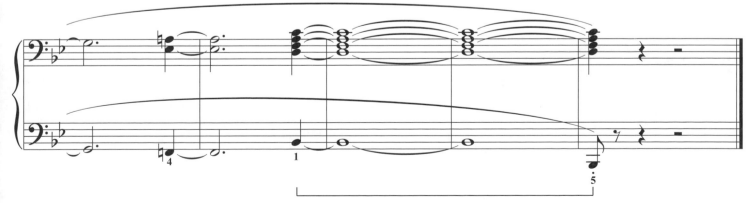

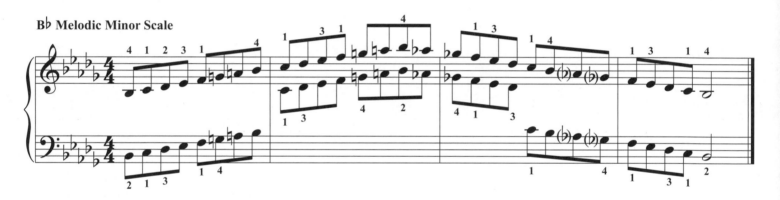

B♭ Melodic Minor Scale

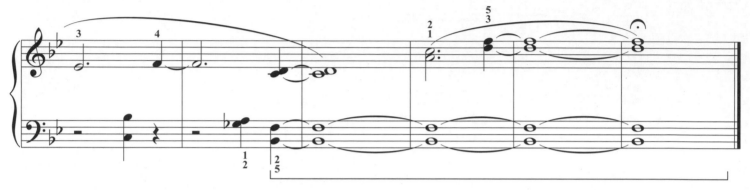

B♭ Melodic Minor Jazz Exercises

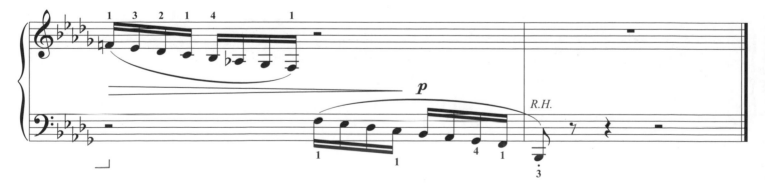

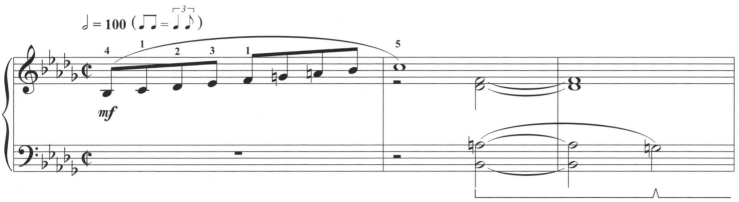

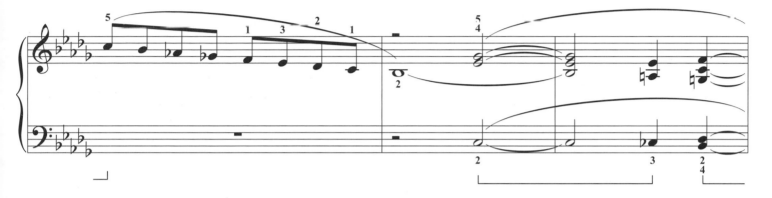

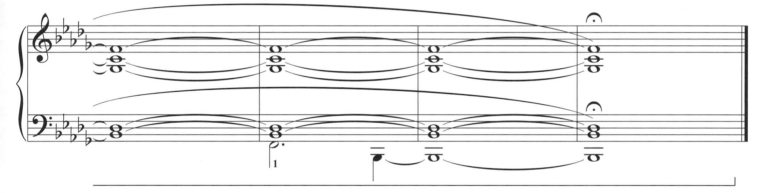

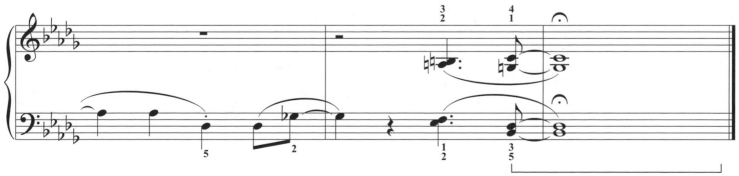

Bb Harmonic Minor Scale

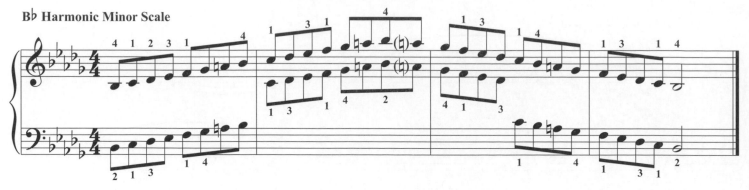

Bb Harmonic Minor Jazz Exercises

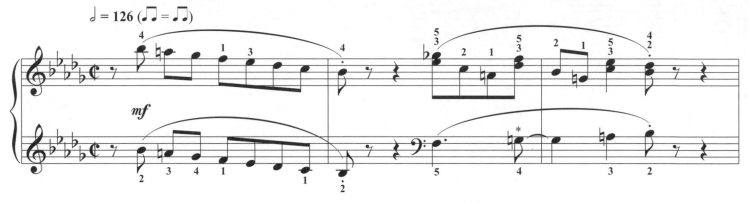

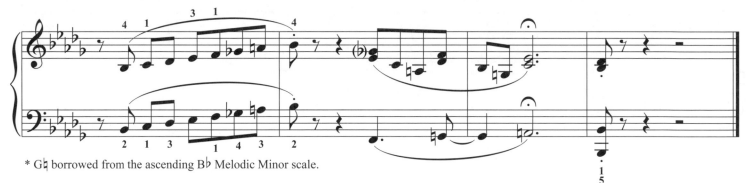

* G♮ borrowed from the ascending Bb Melodic Minor scale.

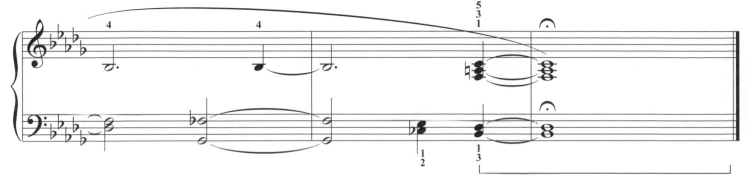

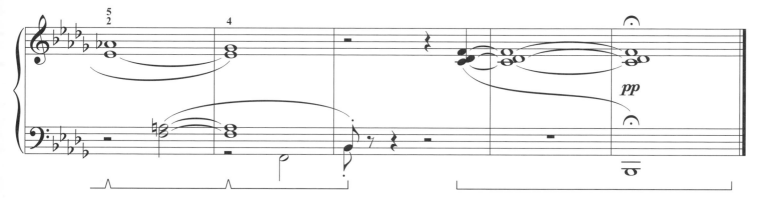

F Major Scale

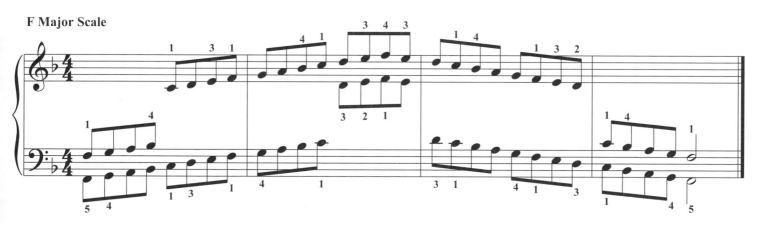

F Major Jazz Exercises

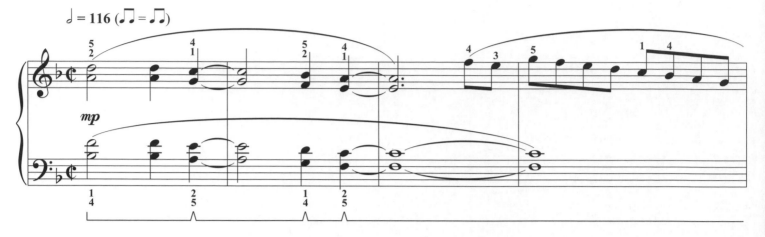

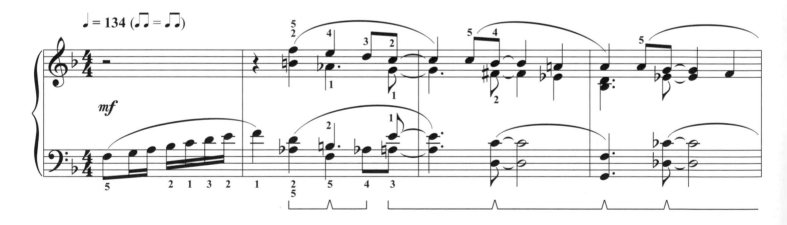

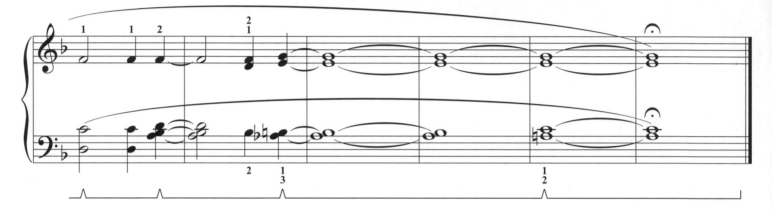

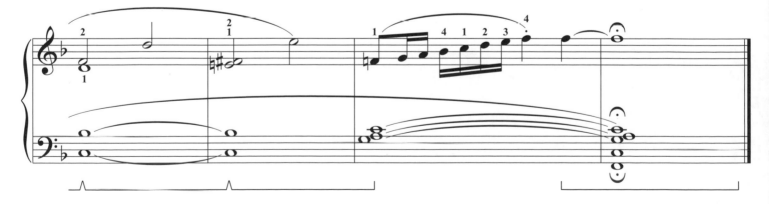

F Melodic Minor Scale

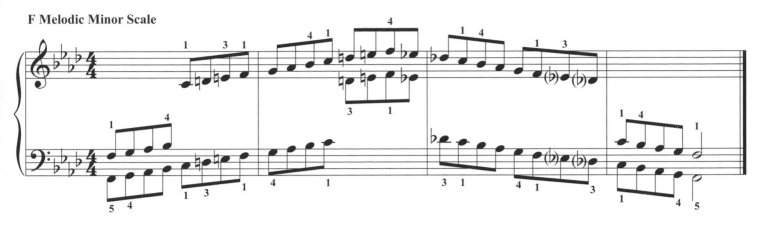

F Melodic Minor Jazz Exercises

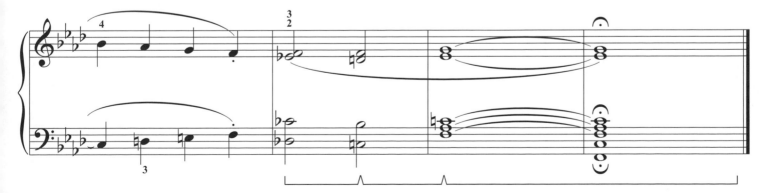

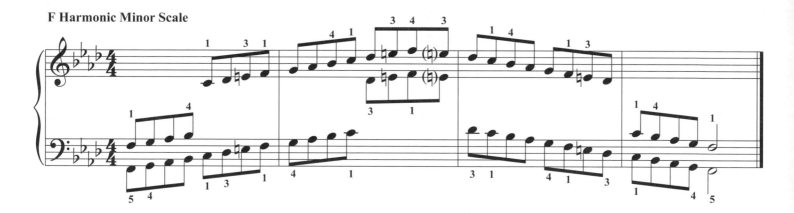

F Harmonic Minor Scale

F Harmonic Minor Jazz Exercises

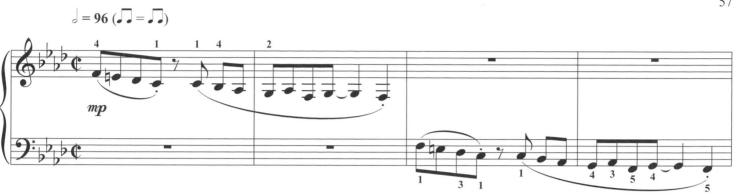

* Octatonic scale (see Appendix)

Note: To complete the Circle of 5ths, return to C major.

APPENDIX

OTHER SCALES EMPLOYED BY JAZZ PIANISTS

Other scales employed at times by jazz pianists include the **chromatic scale**, which features exclusively half-step movement from note to note; the **whole tone scale**, characterized by whole-step movement from note to note; and the **octatonic scale** (also known as the **symmetrical scale** and **diminished scale**), which features alternating half-step/whole-step movement from note to note.

The Octatonic Scale

The octatonic scale consists of eight different pitches of alternating half-steps and whole-steps, the ninth pitch duplicating the first one at the octave. There are three possible different one-octave octatonic scales. (Any other octatonic scale duplicates the pitches of one of the three below.)

Examples:

C-D♭-E♭-E-F♯-G-A-B♭-(C)

C♯-D-E-F-G-A♭-B♭-B-(C♯)

D-E♭-F-G♭-A♭-A-B-C-(D)

There are two possible modalities of the octatonic scale, one that starts with an ascending whole-step, the other with an ascending half-step (see above).

Other Names for the Octatonic Scale

The octatonic scale is also known by two other names:

Symmetrical scale: So named because of the regularity of the arrangement of the scale's intervals (half-step, whole-step, half-step, whole-step, etc.).

Diminished scale: So named because every other pitch of the scale, in combination, outlines a diminished 7th chord. Each one-octave octatonic scale thus possesses the pitches of two different diminished 7th chords.

Example: In the following scale…

C-D♭-E♭-E-F♯-G-A-B♭-(C)

… the two diminished 7th chords (or their enharmonic equivalent pitches) are:

C-E♭-G♭-B♭♭

C♯-E-G-B♭

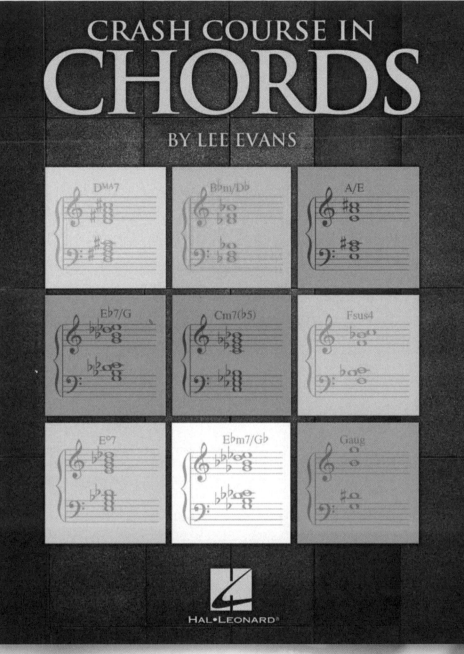